THE SECRET LIFE OF BOO-BOOS

THE SUPER SCIENCE BEHIND HOW YOUR BODY HEALS BUMPS, BRUISES, SCRATCHES, AND SCRAPES!

MARIONA TOLOSA SISTERÉ

sourcebooks
eXplore

A FALL

A KICK

HI, I'M A BOO-BOO!

The playground is my favorite place!
Today I have come with my friends
to play with the kids for a while.

A SCRAPE

It is easy to find other boo-boos at school, in the park,
on trips... Each of your friends probably has at least one.
And there are so many different kinds!

10
9
8
7
6
5
4

WHAT IS BLOOD?

Blood is the red liquid that circulates throughout the body through veins and arteries. It delivers nutrients around the body and collects waste. When we get a boo-boo, the blood rushes to the wound to help it heal and fight infection.

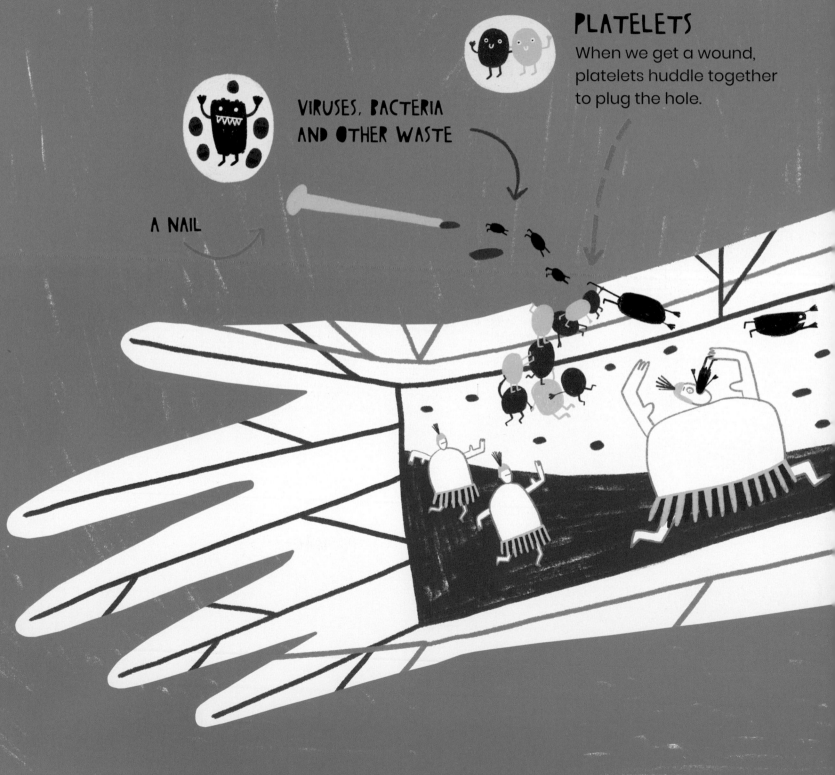

PLATELETS

When we get a wound, platelets huddle together to plug the hole.

VIRUSES, BACTERIA AND OTHER WASTE

A NAIL

RED BLOOD CELLS

They spread nutrients (like oxygen) throughout the body, and clean the body by carrying waste away. They contain a lot of iron, which gives blood its red color.

WHITE BLOOD CELLS

Like gladiators, they fight viruses and bacteria that try to enter the body through wounds. If a boo-boo gets infected, you might notice pus around the wound. This pus is white because it's full of white blood cells that are there to defend your body from the infection.

HOW OUR BODIES HEAL

1 After getting hurt, our skin turns red and painful because blood is pooling behind the boo-boo. Platelets plug the wound so that germs can't get in. When the platelets dry, they form a crust on top of the boo-boo that works like a natural bandage to keep out viruses and bacteria.

2 Meanwhile, the skin and veins are healing with the help of a natural glue in our body known as collagen.

SKIN

COLLAGEN

BLOOD
VESSELS

NUTRIENTS IN

WASTE OUT

3 Underneath the scab, white blood cells continue to fight possible infections. If the wound does become infected, it gets redder, it hurts, and you may notice some white pus around the scab.

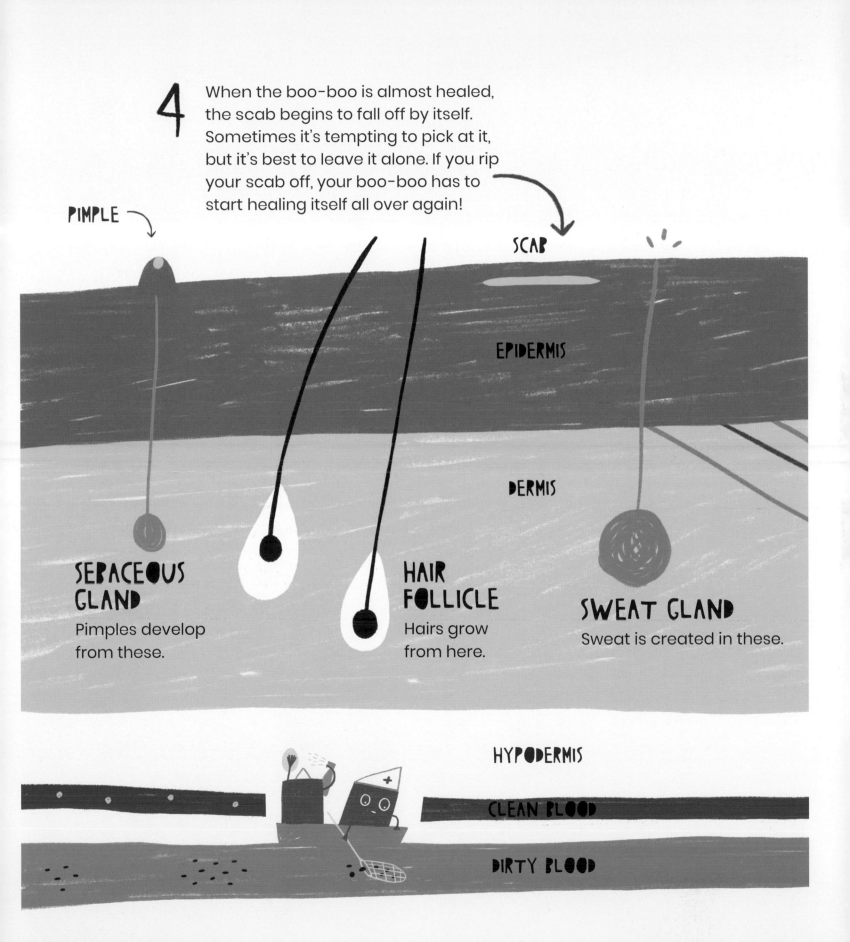

4 When the boo-boo is almost healed, the scab begins to fall off by itself. Sometimes it's tempting to pick at it, but it's best to leave it alone. If you rip your scab off, your boo-boo has to start healing itself all over again!

PIMPLE

SCAB

EPIDERMIS

DERMIS

SEBACEOUS GLAND

Pimples develop from these.

HAIR FOLLICLE

Hairs grow from here.

SWEAT GLAND

Sweat is created in these.

HYPODERMIS

CLEAN BLOOD

DIRTY BLOOD

CATALOG OF BOO-BOOS

There are a lot of different boo-boos, and some of them hurt more than others. Luckily, our skin protects us like bubble wrap, helping us avoid damage in important parts of our body, like muscles, bones, and organs, and keeping viruses and bacteria out!

SCRATCHES

Little bits of skin come off, and a little blood might leak from some very small veins.

WAAAA!

OW!

CUTS

Something sharp breaks through more layers of skin and some bigger veins. Cuts bleed more than scratches.

BUMPS

The veins under the skin break from a very strong blow, but your skin stays intact. The blood that comes out of the broken veins forms bruises under the skin.

OUCH!

BURNS

The outer layers of skin are damaged by too much heat.

IT HURTS!

BITES AND STINGS

A prick to the skin with a kind of poison that causes itching, stinging, or swelling, such as from mosquitoes or nettles.

PUNCTURES

A sharp object pierces the skin. The amount of blood that comes out depends on how many layers of skin the object has broken through.

ITCH ITCH

BASIC FIRST AID

It is very important to treat boo-boos to prevent them from becoming infected.

1 Wash your hands with soap and warm water for twenty seconds.

2 Remove any clothing that is touching or covering the wound.

OOPS!

WASH WASH

3 Wash the wound under a stream of cold water or saline solution. Afterward, gently clean it with gauze moistened with water and soap, always starting from the center and moving outward to the edges.

4 Rinse off the remains of soap and water from the boo-boo.

5 Dry the wound with sterile gauze pads.

YOW!

6 Disinfect the wound, if possible, with a povidone iodine–based disinfectant.

7 If necessary, cover the wound with an adhesive bandage or gauze and tape, pressing gently to slow the bleeding.

8 If the boo-boo won't stop bleeding, it's time to see a doctor, and maybe even get stitches!

THE RAINBOW INSIDE A BRUISE

A bruise, or hematoma, appears when blood gathers under the skin after a hit or blow. The skin swells because blood flows out of broken veins and new blood rushes in to repair them. As it heals, the bruise changes color. But what do the different colors mean?

1 RED

The hit is very recent. Veins have just broken and the skin is reddened because of the blood pooling underneath the surface.

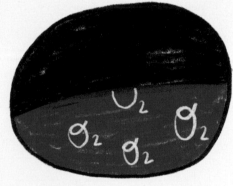

2 BLUE

Blood outside of veins slowly loses its oxygen and turns from red to a bluish color. If the blow hits deep, the bruise may appear blue from the beginning because by the time the blood reaches the top of the skin, it has already lost the oxygen it was carrying.

3 PURPLE

After a few hours or even days, the bruise turns purple because new blood arrives, packed with oxygen-laden red blood cells, ready to help heal the blow. The older bluish blood mixes with the new red blood, creating the purple color you see in your bruise.

4 GREEN

After a few more days, the red blood cells begin to release a substance called hemoglobin, which contains oxygen and iron. As it breaks down, the hemoglobin turns green.

5 YELLOW

When the iron in your red blood cells has almost completely broken down, it turns into bilirubin, a yellow liquid that gives the bruise this color.

BOO-BOOS IN THE WILD

BLISTERS

Wear socks and use lotion to prevent chafing. If you still get a blister, don't try to pop it. Instead, cover it with a bandage specifically for blisters.

SUNBURNS

Put on sunscreen thirty minutes before going out and reapply every two hours, even if it's cloudy.

CUTS ON THE FEET

Water shoes are a great way to avoid injuring your feet on rocks, shells, or pieces of glass that may be hiding in the water.

INSECT BITES

Use bug repellent, especially in hot, humid weather. If a bite itches or stings a lot, ask an adult if you can use hydrocortisone cream or take an antihistamine.

STINGS AND RASHES FROM PLANTS

Even plants can be painful! If your rash hurts or itches, rinse it with cool water, but don't scrub or scratch at it—that can make it feel worse!

JELLYFISH STING

Avoid going in water where there may be jellyfish. If you get stung, clean the sting with seawater and, most importantly, go to the closest first-aid station.

THE WORLD OF BOO-BOOS

MWAH!

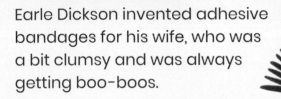

Earle Dickson invented adhesive bandages for his wife, who was a bit clumsy and was always getting boo-boos.

OW!

The Mayans closed wounds by sewing stitches using human hair!

Among the Aztecs, the person in charge of healing wounds—always with natural remedies—was known as the Ticitl.

In the 1800s, leeches were used to suck the blood around a wound and purify it.

According to Ayurveda, or traditional Indian medicine, burns can be healed with a paste made from the licorice plant.

EEK!

Ancient Egyptians covered their wounds very carefully because they believed that evil spirits could enter their bodies through them!

In New Zealand, the Maori use leaves with medicinal properties as wound dressings.

Some African tribes stitch wounds using army ants. The ants' jaws are so strong, they work as an emergency suture.

ANIMAL DOCTORS

Animals are very clever...but usually they can't make their own vet appointments. That's why they've come up with their own ways of taking care of their boo-boos!

MUD

BLECH!

To avoid sunburn,
RHINOCEROSES
use their own natural sunscreen: mud!

LICK LICK

GRIZZLY BEARS

have found the perfect remedy for stings: they chew oshá roots to turn them into a paste with their saliva that soothes the itching.

CATS AND DOGS

lick their wounds because their saliva has antibacterial properties! Their drool helps prevent their wounds from getting infected.

NATURAL REMEDIES

Mother Nature is wise, and can help us heal wounds. For centuries, before adhesive bandages and modern medicines were invented, our ancestors used plants and other natural substances for healing.

BOTANICAL ESSENTIAL OILS

Some flowers work wonders in healing boo-boos. Marigold and lavender reduce inflammation, and eglantine moisturizes and helps heal scars.

HONEY

It's a natural sweetener, but when spread on wounds it helps prevent infections and moisturizes the skin. It also reduces swelling, making boo-boos hurt less.

ONION

It can help disinfect a wound and reduce swelling. A long time ago, the thin skin between onion layers was used as a natural bandage.

ALOE VERA

The goo inside an aloe vera leaf is highly hydrating, it soothes pain from burns, and it helps heal skin.

VINEGAR

It was once used to clean wounds because it can kill some viruses and bacteria.

TURMERIC

This yellow spice reduces inflammation and helps to heal skin naturally.

TRUE OR FALSE

Test your boo-boo knowledge! You can find the answers in the back of this book.

1 You should rip scabs off so that the skin underneath can breathe.

T F

2 Blood tastes metallic because it contains a lot of iron.

T F

3 In a blood donation, a very large amount of blood is removed from the body.

T F

4 Covering a burn with toothpaste helps heal it.

T F

5 You should disinfect a wound with rubbing alcohol.

T F

6 When you get stung by a bee, you should remove the stinger from your skin as soon as possible.

T F

7 Eating lots of oranges can make your scars smaller.

T F

8 If a boo-boo is stinging, that means it is healing.

T F

9 Seawater works well to heal boo-boos.

T F

10 Covering a sunburn with oil or butter soothes the burn and hydrates the skin.

T F

BLOOD

An adult has between 4.5 and 5.5 liters (more than a gallon) of blood in their body! Blood contributes up to 10 percent of an adult's body weight.

ONE DROP OF BLOOD CONTAINS:

WHITE BLOOD CELLS AND PLATELETS

"Clean" (arterial) blood is lighter, brighter, and thinner than "dirty" (venous) blood, which is thicker and darker.

The heart is the motor that helps blood travel all around the body.

RED BLOOD CELLS

Blood is cleaned in the kidneys and liver.

It takes twenty seconds for blood to make its way through the entire body.

PLASMA

This is the liquid that moves blood cells and platelets through the body. It is made up of 90% water.

If you took all your veins and laid them out in a line, they would wrap all the way around the world—twice!

DONATING BLOOD

Platelets last five days because they must be kept at body temperature.

LESS THAN 1%

Red blood cells can survive forty-five days at forty degrees Fahrenheit.

45%

55%

You must eat nutritious food and drink plenty of water before and after donating blood.

In most places, you must be seventeen or older and weigh at least 110 pounds to be able to donate blood.

If you have gotten a tattoo or piercing recently, you might not be allowed to donate blood.

A single donation can save up to three lives!

If it is frozen, plasma can last for three years.

Blood can be donated every fifty-six days. Most donated blood is transfused to cancer patients or people with blood disorders. Donated blood is also used to help patients during surgery or patients who have serious injuries.

TRUE OR FALSE: ANSWERS

 F   1   If you rip a scab off, it not only takes longer to heal, but it makes the wound bigger, which means you'll have a bigger scar.

 T   2   The main component of hemoglobin, which gives blood its red color, is iron.

 F   3   When donating blood, only a pint is extracted, the equivalent of a small bottle of water.

 F   4   Even though toothpaste lowers the temperature of a burn, it seals it and may cause infections. It's better to soak the burn in water (lukewarm or cool, but never with ice) and hydrate it with a burn ointment or aloe vera.

 F   5   Rubbing alcohol may burn the wound and kill the blood cells that are trying to heal it. The best option is a povidone iodine–based disinfectant.

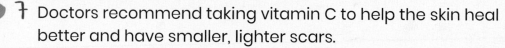 **T**   6   The sooner you remove the stinger, the less it will sting. To remove a bee sting, avoid pulling it, because that can cause it to release more venom. It's best to push it out with the edge of a plastic card, following the direction of the stinger.

 T   7   Doctors recommend taking vitamin C to help the skin heal better and have smaller, lighter scars.

F   8   If a boo-boo starts stinging or itching while it's healing, it may be a sign that it's infected. If you see swelling or redness, see a doctor.

 F   9   Seawater may be contaminated and infect your boo-boos, so make sure to protect them well when you swim at the beach.

 F   10   When you get burned, the most important thing is to lower the temperature of the skin quickly. Fats like oil or butter can trap the heat and make the burn even worse!

First published in the United States in 2021 by Sourcebooks
Text © 2020, 2021 by Ariadna Garcia Turon
Illustrations © 2020, 2021 by Mariona Tolosa Sisteré
Cover and Internal design © 2020, 2021 by Zahorí de Ideas
Cover design by Allison Sundstrom/Sourcebooks
English translation © 2021 by Sourcebooks
Sourcebooks and the colophon are registered trademarks of Sourcebooks.
Published by Sourcebooks eXplore, an imprint of Sourcebooks Kids
P.O. Box 4410, Naperville, Illinois 60567-4410
(630) 961-3900
sourcebookskids.com
Originally published as *La Vida Secreta de las Pupas* in 2020 in Spain by Zahorí de Ideas.
Library of Congress Cataloging-in-Publication Data is on file with the publisher.
Source of Production: 1010 Printing Asia Limited, North Point, Hong Kong, China
Date of Production: January 2021
Run Number: 5020330
Printed and bound in China.
OGP 10 9 8 7 6 5 4 3 2 1